Zoo Math

Zoo Pairs

Patricia Whitehouse

Heinemann Library
Chicago, Illinois

© 2002 Reed Educational & Professional Publishing
Published by Heinemann Library,
an imprint of Reed Educational & Professional Publishing,
Chicago, Illinois

Customer Service 888-454-2279
Visit our website at www.heinemannlibrary.com

Designed by Sue Emerson/Heinemann Library and Ginkgo Creative, Inc.
Printed and bound in the U.S.A. by Lake Book

06 05 04 03 02
10 9 8 7 6 5 4 3 2 1

Library of Congress Cataloging-in-Publication Data
Whitehouse, Patricia, 1958-
   Zoo pairs / Patricia Whitehouse.
       p. cm. — (Zoo math)
Includes index.
Summary: Introduces the mathematical concept of pairs by showing what comes in twos at the zoo.
   ISBN: 1-58810-549-0 (HC), 1-58810-757-4 (Pbk.)
   1. Two (The number)—Juvenile literature. 2. Number concept—Juvenile literature. 3. Counting—Juvenile literature.
   4. Zoo animals—Juvenile literature. [1. Two (The number) 2. Number concept. 3. Counting. 4. Zoo animals.] I. Title.
QA141.3 .W44 2002
513.2'11—dc21

                          2001004900

Acknowledgments
The author and publishers are grateful to the following for permission to reproduce copyright material:
p. 4 Jack Ballard/Visuals Unlimited; pp. 5T, 10, 15 Frans Lanting/Minden Pictures; pp. 5C, 13 Byron Jorjorian; pp. 5B, 6, 17 Dwight Kuhn; p. 7 Tom Stack/Tom Stack & Associates; p. 8 Jim Brandenburg/Minden Pictures; p. 9 Michael P. Turco; p. 10 Stock Photography; p. 12 Barrett & MacKay Photo; p. 14 Gerry Ellis/Minden Pictures; p. 16 Joe McDonald/Tom Stack & Associates; pp. 18, 22 Tui De Roy/Minden Pictures; p. 19 Kennan Ward/Corbis; p. 20 Howie Garber/Wanderlust Images; p. 21 William Dow/Corbis.

Cover photograph by Barrett & MacKay Photo

Every effort has been made to contact copyright holders of any material reproduced in this book. Any omissions will be rectified in subsequent printings if notice is given to the publisher.

Special thanks to our advisory panel for their help in the preparation of this book:

Eileen Day, Preschool Teacher
Chicago, IL

Paula Fischer, K–1 Teacher
Indianapolis, IN

Sandra Gilbert,
Library Media Specialist
Houston, TX

Angela Leeper,
Educational Consultant
North Carolina Department
of Public Instruction
Raleigh, NC

Pam McDonald, Reading Teacher
Winter Springs, FL

Melinda Murphy,
Library Media Specialist
Houston, TX

Helen Rosenberg, MLS
Chicago, IL

Anna Marie Varakin,
Reading Instructor
Western Maryland College

We would like to thank the Brookfield Zoo in Brookfield, Illinois, for reviewing this book for accuracy.

Some words are shown in bold, **like this.**
You can find them in the picture glossary on page 23.

Contents

What Is a Pair?

Two things that match make a pair.

You have a pair of eyes and a pair of feet.

Animals have pairs of eyes and pairs of feet.

What else comes in twos at zoos?

What Has a Pair of Eyes?

A tiger has a pair of eyes.

They are yellow and black.

A snake has a pair of eyes.

They are yellow and black, too.

What Has a Pair of Ears?

An elephant has a pair of ears.

They are big and floppy.

A **camel** has a pair of ears.

They are short and furry.

What Has a Pair of Horns?

A **bighorn sheep** has a pair of horns.

They are big and curly.

A giraffe has a pair of horns.

They are short and bumpy.

What Has a Pair of Antlers?

A **moose** has a pair of **antlers.**

They are wide and flat.

A **reindeer** has a pair of antlers.

They are long and pointed.

What Has a Pair of Legs?

A **flamingo** has a pair of legs.

They are long and thin.

A penguin has a pair of legs.

They are short and fat.

What Has a Pair of Wings?

A **bat** has a pair of wings.

They are covered with thin skin.

A **swan** has a pair of wings.

They are covered with feathers.

What Has Pairs of Flippers?

Sea turtles have two pairs of **flippers**.

There is a front pair and a back pair.

Seals have two pairs of flippers.

You can see this seal's front pair.

What Has Pairs of Paws?

Bears have two pairs of paws.

Here are a **polar bear's** back paws.

Lions have two pairs of paws.

Here are a little lion's front paws.

Quiz

Which pair of legs belongs here?

Look for the answer on page 24.

Picture Glossary

antlers
pages 12–13

flamingo
page 14

reindeer
page 13

bat
page 16

flippers
pages 18–19

seal
page 19

bighorn sheep
page 10

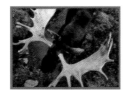

moose
page 12

sea turtle
page 18

camel
page 9

polar bear
page 20

swan
page 17

Note to Parents and Teachers

This book familiarizes children with small sets of like things and the fact that, no matter where they are or what their size, a pair—a set of two—is always the same. You can help children practice this concept by randomly arranging an assortment of pairs, such as shoes, socks, mittens, earrings and so on, on a table. Children can match up the pairs.

As it reinforces a math concept, this book also supports beginning readers. The repeated sentence structure (*A _____ has a pair of _____*) helps children predict the text to come. The two-word change in the sentence on pages 18–21 (*A _____ has two pairs of _____*) offers more fluent readers the challenge of a simple change in the text pattern.

Index

Answer to quiz on page 22

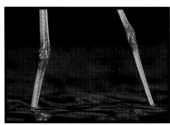

T6